CHAPTER 1

VICKSBURG VICTORY

Americans are locked in a bitter **civil war** in **1863**. Southern states split from the United States of America in 1861, and fighting broke out later that year. In the next two years the battles have gotten bloodier, but neither the **Union army** nor the **Confederate army** can gain an advantage. Leaders on both sides are beginning to realize that winning the war may depend on making the other side's **civilians** feel the pain of war . . .

WHERE WAS THE BATTLE OF VICKSBURG?

OUR WARS

THE **CIVIL WAR** HAS SPLIT THE UNITED STATES. IN **1863** SOLDIERS FROM NORTHERN STATES ARE FIGHTING SOLDIERS FROM SOUTHERN STATES OVER THE ISSUES OF SLAVERY AND STATES' RIGHTS.

IF WE TAKE VICKSBURG, THE WESTERN COUNTRY IS OURS. THIS WAR CAN NOT END UNTIL THAT KEY IS IN OUR POCKET.

VICKSBURG IN ON THE **MISSISSIPPI RIVER**, LONGEST RIVER IN NORTH AMERICA. IN 1863, UNION TROOPS CONTROL NORTHERN AND SOUTHERN ENDS OF THE RIVER. CONFEDERATES CONTROL VICKSBURG.

PRESIDENT LINCOLN, UNION SHIPS CAN'T GET PAST CANNONS AT VICKSBURG.

WE NORTHERN FARMERS CANNOT SELL OUR CROPS IN NEW ORLEANS.

CAPTURE VICKSBURG — OR MAKE PEACE WITH THE CONFEDERATES!!

Gulp!

BROYD '01

GENERAL ULYSSES S. GRANT! LINCOLN WANTS VICKSBURG TAKEN *NOW!*

OH YEAH? WHAT DOES THE PRESIDENT SAY I SHOULD DO ABOUT THOSE **GUNS??**

next: **CANAL STREET**

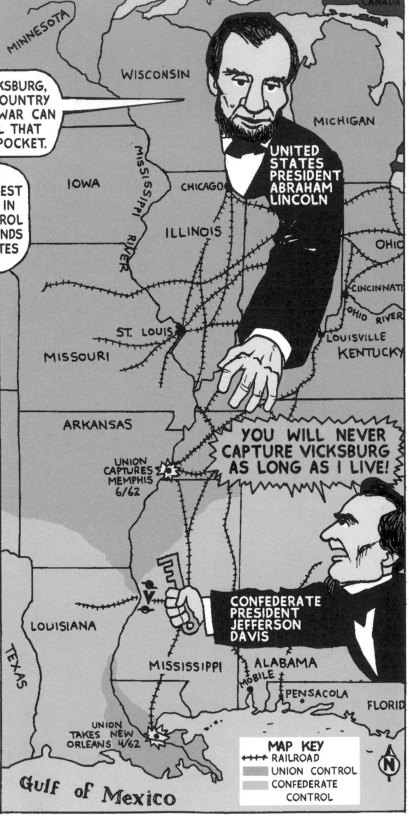

CANADA

MINNESOTA

WISCONSIN

MICHIGAN

IOWA   CHICAGO

UNITED STATES PRESIDENT ABRAHAM LINCOLN

ILLINOIS

OHIO

CINCINNATI

OHIO RIVER

ST. LOUIS

LOUISVILLE

KENTUCKY

MISSOURI

MISSISSIPPI RIVER

ARKANSAS

YOU WILL NEVER CAPTURE VICKSBURG AS LONG AS I LIVE!

UNION CAPTURES MEMPHIS 6/62

V

CONFEDERATE PRESIDENT JEFFERSON DAVIS

LOUISIANA

TEXAS

MISSISSIPPI   ALABAMA

MOBILE   PENSACOLA

FLORIDA

UNION TAKES NEW ORLEANS 4/62

MAP KEY
RAILROAD
UNION CONTROL
CONFEDERATE CONTROL

N

Gulf of Mexico

WHO TRIED TO MOVE THE MISSISSIPPI?

CHESTER AND FIFTH-GRADER SAMUEL ARE HAVING AN 1863 ADVENTURE ON THE MISSISSIPPI RIVER.

SO IN THE **CIVIL WAR**, UNION GUYS REALLY WANT TO TAKE VICKSBURG.

WELL, THEY NEED **SOME** WAY TO GET SHIPS PAST CONFEDERATE CANNONS IN THIS MISSISSIPPI TOWN!

HEY! UNION GENERAL **ULYSSES S. GRANT** HAS HIS TROOPS DIGGING. WHAT'S UP?

THEY WANT A MILE-LONG CANAL AWAY FROM THE GUNS AT VICKSBURG! IF THIS WORKS, UNION SHIPS COULD PASS SAFELY ON THE MISSISSIPPI.

YAZOO RIVER
BLUFFS
MISSISSIPPI RIVER
VICKSBURG
PLANNED CANAL
N

WOOF!

KOFF! GENERAL, RAIN WASHED AWAY THE CANAL AGAIN. THE MEN ARE ALSO GETTING SICK FROM WORKING IN SWAMPS.

YES, **DISEASE** IS A BIG KILLER IN THIS WAR.

IT'S TIME TO ACT. FLAG OFFICER DAVID PORTER, TRY TO SNEAK YOUR SHIPS PAST VICKSBURG TONIGHT!

BOYD '01

UNION SAILORS STACK HAY BALES AND SANDBAGS TO PROTECT THE SHIPS FROM CANNONBALLS. THE SHIPS WILL CARRY SUPPLIES FOR GRANT'S ARMY, NOW MARCHING ON THE WEST SIDE OF THE RIVER. BUT TO **WHERE??**

next: RIVER AND RAILS

HOW DID GRANT ATTACK MISSISSIPPI?

CHESTER, FIFTH-GRADER SAMUEL, AND UNION SHIPS ARE SNEAKING PAST CONFEDERATE CANNONS AT VICKSBURG...

WE'RE ALMOST PAST THE GUNS THAT BLOCK THE MISSISSIPPI RIVER.

OLD MAN RIVERRR...

FOOM

KDOOM

BOOSH

CHESTER!!

OOPS, SORRY.

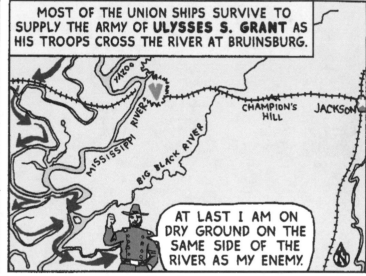

MOST OF THE UNION SHIPS SURVIVE TO SUPPLY THE ARMY OF ULYSSES S. GRANT AS HIS TROOPS CROSS THE RIVER AT BRUINSBURG.

YAZOO MISSISSIPPI RIVER BIG BLACK RIVER CHAMPION'S HILL JACKSON

AT LAST I AM ON DRY GROUND ON THE SAME SIDE OF THE RIVER AS MY ENEMY.

GRANT PUSHES HIS ARMY TO JACKSON.

ARE WE GOING TO CAPTURE VICKSBURG?

WE'RE CUT OFF FROM OUR SUPPLY BOATS ON THE MISSISSIPPI!

TAKE SUPPLIES FROM FARMS WE FIND. I AM BRINGING ONLY MY TOOTHBRUSH!

GRANT'S ARMY CAPTURES JACKSON, THE STATE CAPITAL, IN MAY 1863. BY DESTROYING RAILROADS THERE, GRANT STOPS CONFEDERATES FROM MOVING TROOPS OR SUPPLIES QUICKLY.

CONFEDERATE SOLDIERS MARCH EAST FROM VICKSBURG TO STOP GRANT. IN BATTLE AT CHAMPION'S HILL, CONFEDERATES LOSE ABOUT 4,000 MEN AND 27 CANNONS.

next: SIEGE

4

HOW WAS VICKSBURG PROTECTED?

IN THE **CIVIL WAR**, ON APRIL 19, 1863, **ULYSSES S. GRANT'S** UNION SOLDIERS ATTACK **VICKSBURG** ON THE **MISSISSIPPI RIVER**.

CONFEDERATE SOLDIERS HAVE BUILT DIRT FORTS AROUND THE CITY. THIS IS HARD TO CLIMB!

BBOYD'01

THEY ALSO PUT TRAPS OF SHARP STICKS! POINTY!! COME ON, MEN!

ACTUALLY, THIS SOLDIER IS **NOT** A MAN. IT IS JENNIE HODGERS, WHO DISGUISES HERSELF SO SHE CAN FIGHT IN MANY BATTLES!

OWIE!

THE UNION ATTACK FAILS. GRANT ORDERS ANOTHER CHARGE THREE DAYS LATER. IT ALSO FAILS.

THE REBELS HAVE DUG IN TOO WELL. WE MUST STARVE THEM. *START THE SIEGE!*

YES, GENERAL GRANT!

Uh oh...

KBOOM

next: THE BATCAVE

5

WHY DID VICKSBURG SURRENDER?

On the Civil War, Union soldiers blast away for seven weeks at **VICKSBURG** on the **MISSISSIPPI RIVER**.

Vicksburg's people are trapped in a real world SURVIVOR

People in Vicksburg dig caves.

BOOMFOOMAZOOM

MAMA, IT IS SCARY OUT THERE.

IT'S SCARY IN HERE, TOO! SNAKE!

No supplies get through Union lines to the townspeople or Confederate soldiers. People begin to eat dogs, mules, and...

SHAVOOM

BOOVOOM

And no reinforcements are coming. Many soldiers went east to help General **ROBERT E. LEE** invade the North. I wonder what is happening in **GETTYSBURG**?

Many southern soldiers die of **DISEASES** they catch from being tired and hungry. When they get too weak to fight, they surrender **JULY 4, 1863**.

Vicksburg's people are so mad at being beaten that they will not celebrate July 4 (America's birthday) for 82 years.

The Union victory at Vicksburg splits the South. Since the Union controls all of the Mississippi, Union supplies move quickly and rebel supplies don't.

AHHHHH, "THE FATHER OF WATERS" AGAIN GOES UNVEXED TO THE SEA.

HEY, **PRESIDENT LINCOLN**, LESS TALKING, MORE ROWING!

END

CHAPTER 2

GETTYSBURG

Confederate General Robert E. Lee sees the North's grip tightening on his supplies. The **Union's blockade of Southern ports** such as **Savannah**, **Charleston**, and **New Orleans** is keeping European supply ships from helping his soldiers – and helping Southern people at home. So a year after his first, failed attempt to invade the North, Lee heads north again, into **Pennsylvania**. Maybe a big victory there will make Europe support the South's independence and make Northerners ask for peace . . .

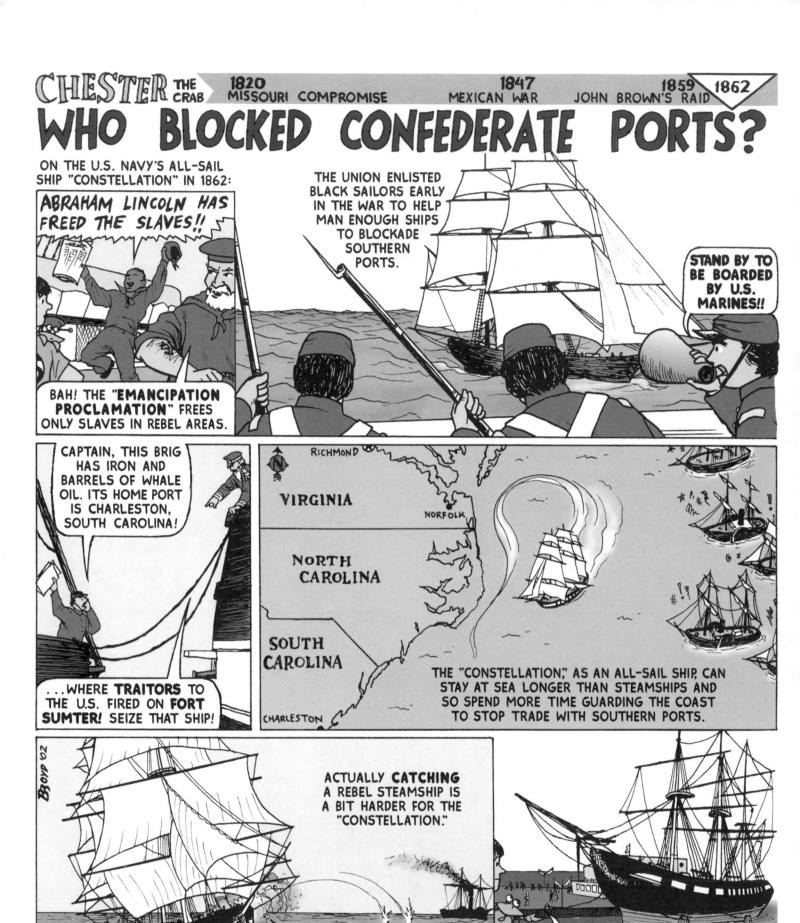

WHAT HAPPENED TO "STONEWALL"?

AT THE BEGINNING OF THE CIVIL WAR, THE UNION USES ITS CAVALRY TROOPS TO GUARD SUPPLY WAGONS AND CAMPS.

THE CONFEDERATES SEND J.E.B. STUART'S CAVALRY ON SWIFT RAIDS BEHIND ENEMY LINES TO CAPTURE MUCH-NEEDED SUPPLIES.

GRAB THAT GUN AMMO!!

WITH NO AIRPLANES OR SATELLITES INVENTED YET, THE BEST WAY TO DISCOVER THE ENEMY IS TO RIDE AS NEAR HIM AS POSSIBLE. CONFEDERATE GENERAL THOMAS "STONEWALL" JACKSON USES CAVALRY VERY WELL.

STUART, HAVE YOU FOUND ANYTHING?

YES. WE CAN SURPRISE THE ENEMY BY SNEAKING THROUGH THIS "WILDERNESS" NEAR **CHANCELLORSVILLE**.

ON MAY 2, **1863**, JACKSON'S 28,000 MEN ATTACK AT SUNDOWN AND WHIP UNION TROOPS COOKING DINNER. THIS IS THE **BATTLE OF CHANCELLORSVILLE, VA.**

THE TWO ARMIES MIX. THAT NIGHT JACKSON RIDES IN THE WOODS TO FIND THE NEW BATTLE LINE BETWEEN THE ARMIES.

HE FINDS IT. SOME OF HIS OWN FRONTLINE SOLDIERS SHOOT HIM, THINKING HE IS A YANKEE.

A DOCTOR CUTS OFF JACKSON'S WOUNDED ARM. **GENERAL ROBERT E. LEE** IS UPSET.

"STONEWALL" HAS LOST HIS LEFT ARM, BUT I HAVE LOST MY RIGHT.

JACKSON GETS PNEUMONIA AND DIES MAY 10. THE SOUTH LOSES ONE OF ITS BEST GENERALS.

ARM OF STONEWALL JACKSON MAY 3, 1863

next: GETTYSBURG, PA.

WHY WAS THE FIGHTING AT GETTYSBURG?

ROBERT E. LEE COMMANDS THE CONFEDERATE ARMY IN THE **CIVIL WAR**...

J.E.B. STUART IS "THE EYES OF THE ARMY." HE TELLS ME WHEN AND WHERE UNION TROOPS ARE MOVING. STUART HAS NEVER BROUGHT ME FALSE INFORMATION.

BLOYD '00

BUT UNION CAVALRY SOLDIERS ON HORSEBACK SURPRISE STUART'S HORSEMEN ON JUNE 9, **1863**, AT BRANDY STATION, VIRGINIA.

THOSE YANKEES EMBARRASSED ME!!

GENERAL STUART, WE'RE INVADING PENNSYLVANIA. FOOL THE YANKS BY BOTHERING THEIR CAMPS ELSEWHERE.

PENNSYLVANIA
MARYLAND
BALTIMORE
POTOMAC RIVER
VIRGINIA
WASHINGTON D.C.

oh, I WILL BOTHER THEM **BIGTIME!**

JUNE 28:

GOOD JOB! WE CAPTURED 400 UNION SOLDIERS AND 125 WAGONS AROUND ROCKVILLE.

JUNE 30...

WHERE **IS** STUART?

I DON'T KNOW. I ALSO DON'T KNOW HOW CLOSE THE UNION ARMY IS. WELL, LET'S KEEP GOING **NORTH**...

WHERE IN BLAZES IS STUART?!!

THE UNION AND CONFEDERATE ARMIES STUMBLE INTO EACH OTHER AT GETTYSBURG. FOR THREE HOT JULY DAYS THEY FIGHT IN BRUTAL, MAN-TO-MAN COMBAT.

next: **HIGHER GROUND**

WHY DO WE HAVE MEMORIAL DAY?

THE BATTLE OF GETTYSBURG

IS THE TURNING POINT IN THE CIVIL WAR. THE UNION HOLDS THE ADVANTAGE IN THIS THREE-DAY FIGHT BECAUSE IT HAS THE **HIGH GROUND** AROUND GETTYSBURG. IT'S EASY TO SHOOT DOWN AT MEN STRUGGLING TO CLIMB A HILL ON A HOT JULY DAY.

ON JULY 3, GENERAL GEORGE PICKETT SENDS 15,000 REBEL TROOPS ACROSS AN OPEN FIELD TO CEMETERY RIDGE. UNION FIRE EASILY CUTS **"PICKETT'S CHARGE"** TO PIECES.

ABOUT 50,000 PEOPLE ARE KILLED OR WOUNDED AT GETTYSBURG. ABOUT 28,000 OF THOSE ARE FROM **CONFEDERATE GENERAL ROBERT E. LEE'S** ARMY. HIS WEAKENED ARMY MUST RETREAT TO VIRGINIA.

FOUR MONTHS LATER, **U.S. PRESIDENT ABRAHAM LINCOLN** DEDICATES A GETTYSBURG CEMETERY FOR THE UNION SOLDIERS.

Four score and seven years ago, our fathers brought forth upon this continent a new nation, conceived in liberty and dedicated to the proposition that all men are created equal.

LINCOLN'S SPEECH IS THE **GETTYSBURG ADDRESS.** HE SAYS THE UNION SOLDIERS DIED TO KEEP ONE NATION WITH A GOVERNMENT **"OF** THE PEOPLE, **BY** THE PEOPLE, **FOR** THE PEOPLE."

THE NEXT YEAR EMMA HUNTER DECORATES THE GRAVE OF HER DAD, WHO FOUGHT AT GETTYSBURG. SHE INSPIRES OTHERS TO DECORATE SOLDIERS' GRAVES. THIS PRACTICE EVENTUALLY LEADS TO THE NATIONAL HOLIDAY CALLED **MEMORIAL DAY.**

next: home fires

HOW DID THE CIVIL WAR HURT PEOPLE?

AFTER LOSING AT GETTYSBURG, ROBERT E. LEE AND THE CONFEDERATE SOLDIERS RETURN TO VIRGINIA. SOUTHERNERS FEEL THE PAIN OF THE WAR RETURNING TO THEIR SOIL. BATTLES TEAR UP SOUTHERN FARMS AND LIVES. HARSH CONDITIONS ON THE HOMEFRONT LEAD TO DEATH FROM DISEASE AND EXPOSURE. BUT SOUTHERNERS CONTINUE TO SUPPORT THE WAR...

THIS WAR IS COSTING US ALL DEARLY. IT WILL GET EVEN WORSE, I'M AFRAID.

FATHER, I'M JOINING THE CONFEDERATE ARMY.

ME TOO, DAD!

ME TOO!

ME TOOW!

WAR!

NO YOU DON'T!

WILLIAM BYRD HARRISON IS RIGHT. ONE OF HIS SONS IS KILLED AND ANOTHER LOSES HIS LEG IN THE WAR.

AND IN 1864 THE WAR COMES TO HIS VIRGINIA FARM ON THE JAMES RIVER.

THOOM

HEE HEE! TARGET PRACTICE!

KISH!

SMASH!

UNION MEN MOVING ON THE RIVER STOP AT THE PLANTATION FOR SUPPLIES. UPPER BRANDON IS AN EASY TARGET BECAUSE HARRISON HAS MOVED TO WESTERN VIRGINIA FOR SAFETY.

THIS DESTRUCTION IS PART OF THE UNION ARMY'S STRATEGY OF "TOTAL WAR." IT TRIES TO DESTROY AS MUCH VIRGINIA FARMLAND AS POSSIBLE.

A FEW MONTHS LATER **UNION GENERAL ULYSSES S. GRANT** CROSSES THE JAMES NEAR UPPER BRANDON ON HIS WAY TO ATTACK **RICHMOND**, THE CAPITAL OF THE CONFEDERACY. HARRISON'S FARM IS A MESS. VIRGINIA RAILROADS ARE RIPPED UP, CROPS ARE DEAD, AND SLAVES ARE FREED BUT OWN NO LAND OR WAY TO PLANT NEW CROPS...

END

ATLANTA BURNING

After the Confederates lose Gettysburg, the Union can confidently take the warfare into the South again. **The Southern troops left to fight are becoming younger and more poorly equipped and clothed.** But they still fight fiercely. **United States General William T. Sherman** decides he must destroy **Atlanta**, "the crossroads of the Confederacy," to convince Southerners to give up this terrible war. . .

WHEN DID THE UNION CAPTURE ATLANTA?

UNION SOLDIERS SHELL ATLANTA IN **1864** DURING THE **CIVIL WAR**.

There is a fire in town every day. The shelling gets worse and worse. I wish something would make it stop!

ON AUGUST 26, AFTER ALMOST TWO WEEKS OF BOMBING. . .

LISTEN!

WHAT? I DON'T HEAR ANYTHING.

THAT'S JUST IT: THE SHELLING STOPPED!

THE YANKEES LEFT THEIR CAMPSITES!

WE SHOWED 'EM WE COULD OUTLAST THEM!!

I'LL BET THEY ARE RUNNING BACK TO TENNESSEE!

NO, NOT GOING **NORTH** TO TENNESSEE . . .

SNEAKING AROUND TO THE **SOUTH** SIDE OF ATLANTA.

CUT THESE RAILROAD LINES THAT BRING SUPPLIES TO THE CITY.

WHEN THE CONFEDERATES REALIZE THEY ARE SURROUNDED, THEY SEND 24,000 SOLDIERS AT THE UNION LINES!

IN TWO DAYS OF FIGHTING, THIS FORCE IS CUT TO 5,000 MEN. ON SEPTEMBER 1, THE REST OF THE SOUTHERN ARMY LEAVES ATLANTA.

THE UNION ARMY MARCHES INTO ATLANTA ON SEPT. 2, 1864.

THIS VICTORY SILENCES LOUD CRITICS OF PRESIDENT ABRAHAM LINCOLN. HE WINS REELECTION EASILY BECAUSE IT NOW SEEMS THE UNION WILL WIN.

next: HOT-LANTA

WHERE WAS "SHERMAN'S MARCH TO THE SEA?"

After burning Atlanta, Union General William T. Sherman cuts loose from his own supply lines. His soldiers eat food from Georgia's farmland, then destroy the farms and railroads and move on.

THE ENTIRE SOUTH — MAN, WOMAN, AND CHILD — IS AGAINST US. WE MUST MAKE OLD AND YOUNG, RICH AND POOR, FEEL THE HARD HAND OF WAR. THE MORE AWFUL WE MAKE WAR, THE SOONER IT WILL END.

TENNESSEE

CHATTANOOGA

NORTH CAROLINA

CHARLOTTE

MARCHING 15 MILES A DAY, SHERMAN'S ARMY DESTROYS AN AREA 50 MILES WIDE AND 300 MILES LONG.

SOUTH CAROLINA

GEORGIA

ATLANTA

ALABAMA

GEORGIA SLAVES JOIN SHERMAN'S MARCH, CHEERING THEIR FREEDOM.

GEORGIA'S FARMS ARE DEFENDED BY OLD MEN AND TEENAGE BOYS — NO MATCH FOR SHERM'S ARMY.

CHARLESTON

Atlantic Ocean

MEANWHILE, 40,000 CONFEDERATE SOLDIERS GO NORTH TO ATTACK NASHVILLE, TENNESSEE, TO TRY TO DISTRACT SHERMAN. UNION TROOPS IN TENNESSEE CUT THE REBELS TO PIECES.

ON DECEMBER 21, 1864, SHERMAN CAPTURES SAVANNAH, GEORGIA. UNION SHIPS ARE WAITING WITH FRESH SUPPLIES.

SAVANNAH

BOYD '04

SAVANNAH IS MY CHRISTMAS PRESENT TO PRESIDENT ABRAHAM LINCOLN.

HO HO HOTSHOT!

END

CHAPTER 4

RICHMOND FALLS

Combat in the Civil War is often brutal, man-to-man fighting. But **United States General Ulysses S. Grant** knows the North has more people than the South and so can replace the soldiers it loses on the battlefield. He presses south to **Richmond** and lays siege to the near-by railroad hub at Petersburg, Virginia. Grant waits months for the Confederate army to weaken further. . .

HOW DID THE CIVIL WAR FINISH?

WAIT, CHESTER, YOUR STORY ABOUT **JEFFERSON DAVIS** LEFT OUT THE FUNNIEST PART. MY DAD SAYS HE WAS CAPTURED WEARING A **DRESS**!!

IF YOU WANT THAT KIND OF DETAIL, LET'S LOOK MORE CLOSELY AT THE END OF AMERICA'S CIVIL WAR...

BBOYD '03

IN THE SPRING OF **1864** THE UNION ARMY HAS A NEW PLAN FROM A NEW GENERAL: **ULYSSES S. GRANT.**

SIR, 50,000 OF OUR SOLDIERS HAVE BEEN KILLED OR WOUNDED IN THE LAST MONTH! WE **MUST** RETREAT!

NO! CONFEDERATES LOST 32,000 MEN. **WE CAN REPLACE OUR SOLDIERS; THEY CAN'T. ATTACK AGAIN!!**

SOUTHERN SOLDIERS DEFEND **RICHMOND**, THE **CAPITAL OF THE CONFEDERACY.** GRANT GOES SOUTH, CROSSING THE JAMES RIVER.

WHAT IS GRANT'S GOAL?

I HEAR WE ARE ATTACKING PETERSBURG. FIVE RAILROADS MEET THERE. IT'S THE SUPPLY BASE FOR THE CONFEDERATES.

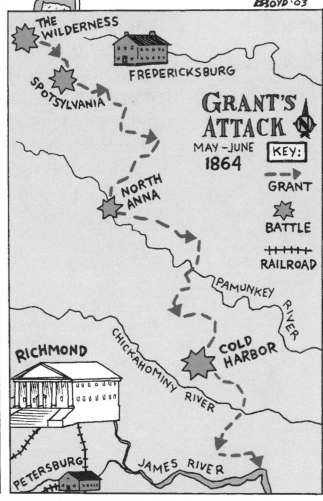

THE WILDERNESS

FREDERICKSBURG

SPOTSYLVANIA

GRANT'S ATTACK
MAY – JUNE 1864

NORTH ANNA

KEY:
- - - > GRANT
✶ BATTLE
+++++ RAILROAD

PAMUNKEY RIVER

RICHMOND

CHICKAHOMINY RIVER

COLD HARBOR

PETERSBURG

JAMES RIVER

ABOUT 14,000 CONFEDERATE SOLDIERS STOP 80,000 UNION MEN AT PETERSBURG! THE UNION ARMY DELAYS JUST LONG ENOUGH FOR **CONFEDERATE GENERAL ROBERT E. LEE'S** MEN TO JOIN THIS FIGHT.

next: **CRATER FACE**

WHO GOT PINNED IN PETERSBURG?

THE TWO MAIN ARMIES IN THE **CIVIL WAR** ARE TIRED IN JUNE **1864**. THEY FACE EACH OTHER AT PETERSBURG, VIRGINIA. **SOUTHERN GENERAL ROBERT E. LEE** SAYS:

> I HAVE BEEN WINNING THE RUNNING BATTLES ACROSS VIRGINIA. BUT NOW I MUST SIT HERE TO DEFEND MY **LAST** SUPPLY DEPOT. **NOT** GOOD.

GRITS, CORNMEAL, CHEERY-OS, SYRUP, CHICKEN FINGERS, KETCHUP, CHEE...

> LEE IS DUG IN TOO WELL. WE CAN LAY SIEGE TO HIS ARMY AND STARVE THEM OUT, LIKE I DID LAST YEAR TO **VICKSBURG**, MISSISSIPPI.

BOTH SIDES DIG MILES OF TRENCHES FOR PROTECTION.

> I'VE SEEN STUFF LIKE THIS IN WAR PICTURES BEFORE.

> TRENCHES SHOW UP IN WORLD WAR I.

THE YANKEES DIG LONGER TRENCHES TO FORCE THE CONFEDERATES TO SPREAD OUT ACROSS 35 MILES TO BLOCK THEM.

WHAT?

> I HATE THE GAME "TELEPHONE!"

SOME UNION TROOPS ARE MINERS FROM PENNSYLVANIA.

> HEY! WE COULD TUNNEL **UNDER** THE CONFEDERATE LINES AND BLOW THEM UP!

THEY DIG, AND IN THE EARLY MORNING OF JULY 30, 1864...

next: **Richmond Falls**

UNION SOLDIERS HAVE TROUBLE CRAWLING ACROSS THE BIG CRATER CREATED BY THE BLAST. THE SOUTHERN LINE HOLDS.

BOYD '03

WHEN DID RICHMOND FINALLY FALL?

IN THE **1864** STANDOFF NEAR PETERSBURG, VIRGINIA, CONFEDERATE TROOPS RUN LOW ON SUPPLIES. FALL TURNS TO WINTER.

THAT LOOKS LIKE WHAT SLAVES GOT FOR MEALS ON SOUTHERN PLANTATIONS BEFORE THE WAR...

YEAH— A CUP OF CORNMEAL AND RATTY BACON.

UNION TROOPS GET PLENTY OF SHELLS AND SANDWICHES FROM UNION SHIPS COMING UP THE JAMES RIVER.

CONFEDERATE GENERAL ROBERT E. LEE SAYS:

I HAVE SPOKEN TO OUR CONGRESS IN RICHMOND, 35 MILES AWAY. THEY DO NOTHING BUT EAT PEANUTS AND CHEW TOBACCO, WHILE MY MEN STARVE.

UNION GENERAL PHIL SHERIDAN JOINS IN MARCH 1865.

SHERIDAN WINS THE FIVE FORKS AREA ON APRIL 1. THIS CUTS THE LAST SUPPLY LINE TO LEE'S ARMY.

PULL OUR MEN BACK TO THE NORTH SIDE OF THE APPOMATTOX RIVER. TELL OFFICIALS TO PICK A NEW CAPITAL OF THE CONFEDERACY — WE CANNOT DEFEND RICHMOND.

KEY:
++++ RAILROAD
◄ UNION ATTACK
▭ LEE'S ARMY

CONFEDERATE PRESIDENT JEFFERSON DAVIS GETS THE BAD NEWS AT CHURCH ON APRIL 2.

MAYBE WE CAN MEET OUR OTHER SOLDIERS IN NORTH CAROLINA AND KEEP FIGHTING?

DAVIS BOARDS A TRAIN GOING SOUTH TO DANVILLE, VIRGINIA. IT STARTS AT 11 P.M. AS RICHMOND BURNS FROM FIRES SET BY RETREATING REBELS.

next: R.R. TIES

HOW WAS JEFFERSON DAVIS CAUGHT?

JEFFERSON DAVIS RUNS THE **CONFEDERATE STATES OF AMERICA** FROM DANVILLE, VIRGINIA, FOR A WEEK IN **APRIL 1865.**

WE MUST HAVE SUPPLIES READY FOR **GENERAL ROBERT E. LEE** WHEN HIS ARMY GETS HERE. I'VE...

MR. PRESIDENT.!!

LEE HAS SURRENDERED AT **APPOMATTOX!**

SUTHERLIN HOUSE

PACK UP — WE'RE GOING TO GREENSBORO, NORTH CAROLINA!

LATE IN THE NIGHT OF APRIL 10, DAVIS AND THE CONFEDERATE GOVERNMENT HEAD SOUTH.

MAYBE WE FORM AN ARMY IN TEXAS?

DAVIS LEARNS THAT UNITED STATES PRESIDENT **ABRAHAM LINCOLN** HAS BEEN KILLED.

OUTLAW!

$100,000

WH-- NORTHERNERS THINK I PLOTTED LINCOLN'S MURDER??!

GENERAL JOSEPH JOHNSTON GIVES UP APRIL 26. **STILL** DAVIS RUNS HIS "GOVERNMENT BY THE ROADSIDE."

ALL THOSE IN FAVOR OF VISITING **FLORIDA?**

UNION TROOPS FIND THE DAVIS CAMP NEAR IRWINVILLE, **GEORGIA,** ON MAY 10.

DAVIS TRIES TO ESCAPE THROUGH THE WOODS, COVERED BY HIS WIFE'S SHAWL. HE IS CAPTURED.

THE ARMY PUTS DAVIS IN FORT MONROE IN VIRGINIA AND HE STAYS FOR TWO YEARS BECAUSE HE REFUSES TO ADMIT HE DID ANYTHING WRONG AS PRESIDENT OF THE CONFEDERACY.

THE FEDERAL GOVERNMENT RELEASES DAVIS IN MAY 1867. HE DIES IN **1889,** HAVING NEVER REGAINED HIS CITIZENSHIP IN THE UNITED STATES. **END**